Getting Your Child Ready for Outpatient Surgery

Jerry C. Vaughan
Photos by Paul Griffen
Illustrations by McCall Vaughan

For Susan, Christopher, Wilson, and McCall

- JCV

Dedicated to Julie Ann Paschal

Now may the God of hope fill you with all the joy
and peace in believing, that you may abound
in hope by the power of the Holy Spirit.

Romans 15:13

1

Printed in the United States of America
by Kensho Printing Company, Nashville, TN, 2004
Graphic Design: Wendi K. Powell, Kairos Designs, Nashville, TN
Project Coordinator: Leanne Hance

Library of Congress Catalog Number: 2004104729
ISBN# 0-615-12554-9

Introduction

Across America every day, more than 6,000 surgeries are performed on children. ***Getting Your Child Ready for Outpatient Surgery*** was written to give children a positive, educational, and enlightened understanding of the surgical experience they will encounter. Most children who are having surgery for the first time are uncertain of what lies ahead after leaving the comfort of their own home. Parents try to explain the surgical experience to their children in the best way possible. Children naturally react to a hospital visit like they would visiting their pediatrician or Ear, Nose, and Throat specialist. They are terrified of getting a shot or being examined when it is very uncomfortable.

Getting Your Child Ready for Outpatient Surgery can give children a step-by-step guide to understanding their outpatient surgical experience. In the following pages, the child will be taken from the admitting area to discharge in detail. Each area of the outpatient surgery center will be covered and presented in a nurturing way to the child. This detailed description of the outpatient surgical experience can provide children with information they can understand and will, hopefully, make their surgery day a little brighter.

Your child will enjoy the colorful illustrations drawn by an eight-year old patient following her first outpatient surgery. These illustrations truly show how much a child can comprehend during their first time surgical experience.

Outpatient Surgery Center

When you and your mom and dad visited the doctor, he or she told you about a place where you will have surgery (an operation) to make you feel much better. The building where you will have your surgery is called an outpatient surgery center. An outpatient surgery center is a place where doctors, nurses, and many other people work to help children and grownups feel better when they are having surgery. The outpatient surgery center can be located either inside the hospital building or away from the hospital. It is called an outpatient surgery center because you have surgery and go home all in the same day.

New Friends

When you arrive at the outpatient surgery center, you will meet many new friends that will be taking care of you. The doctors, nurses, and the rest of the staff can take care of many people at the same time. Your mom, dad, or special friend that brings you to the outpatient surgery center can stay with you while you are there. The first place you will go is the Admitting Area.

Admitting Area

The first stop at the outpatient surgery center will be the Admitting Area. Your mom, dad, or special friend will answer questions about your health and fill out some papers for your visit. You will be given a plastic bracelet to put on your wrist. The bracelet will have your name printed on it. Lots of people that work in the outpatient surgery center will look at your bracelet while you are there. This will help the staff make sure they call you by the correct name. The next stop for you will be checking in your pre-operative room. Let's go to your pre-operative room and meet the nurses and other people that will be taking good care of you during your surgery.

Your Room at the Outpatient Surgery Center

After you receive your name bracelet, you and your mom, dad, or special friend will be taken to the pre-operative area to check into your room. Your mom, dad, or special friend will be able to stay with you in your room before your surgery. Next, you will meet your nurse friends who will help take care of you. They will help you get ready for surgery. All the nurses, doctors, and staff members you meet will be your friends and helpers while you visit the outpatient surgery center.

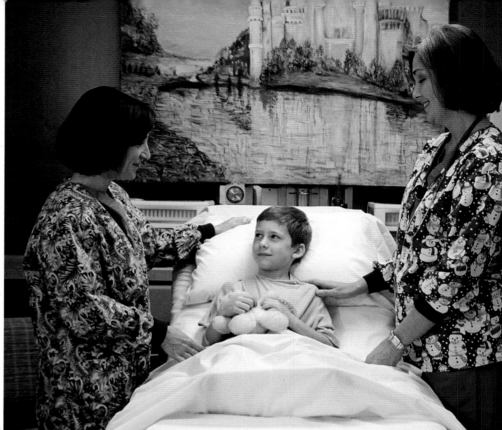

Getting Ready for Surgery

Now that you have met your nurse friends, they will begin getting you ready for surgery. You will be asked to put on a patient gown that will be worn during your surgery. Your mom, dad, or special friend can help you put on your patient gown. The gown ties in the back and is very comfortable. After you put on your gown, your nurse friends will run some tests that your doctor has asked them to do before your surgery. You will probably be familiar with lots of these tests, because your pediatrician usually does these during checkups. Let's talk about the tests that might be done.

First, your nurse friend will need to figure your height. You will stand on a scale to measure how tall you are…

... and how much you weigh.

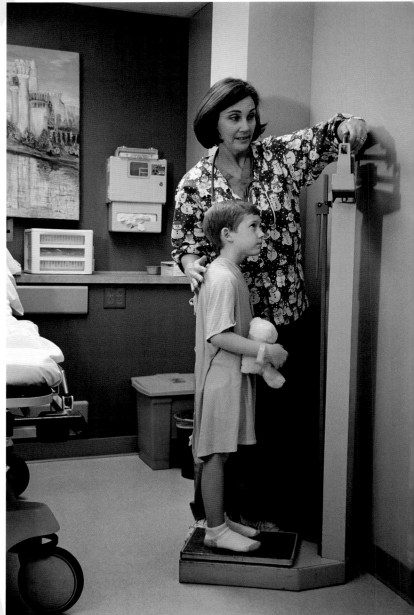

Next, your nurse friend will take your temperature with a thermometer…

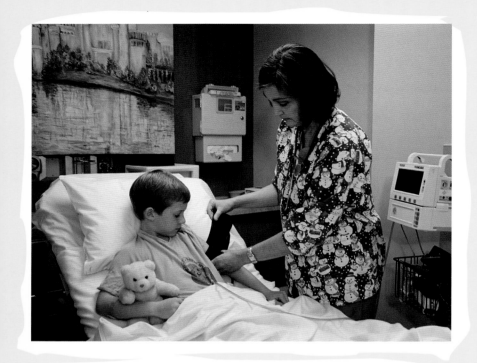

... and then check your blood pressure by wrapping a blood pressure cuff around your arm. When the cuff gets tight on your arm, you may feel a squeeze, but it doesn't hurt. Checking your blood pressure can tell your doctor how well your heart is sending blood through your body.

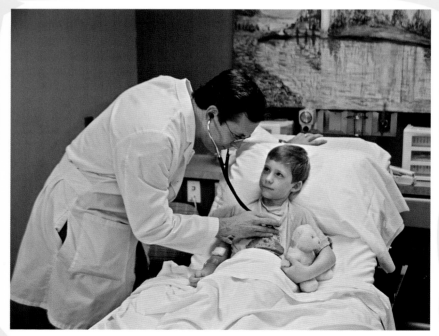

Next, your doctor or nurse will use a stethoscope to listen to your breathing and heartbeat. They will be able to hear how the air is moving in and out of your lungs, and if your heart is beating in a regular pattern. The stethoscope may feel cold at first, but will quickly warm up ...

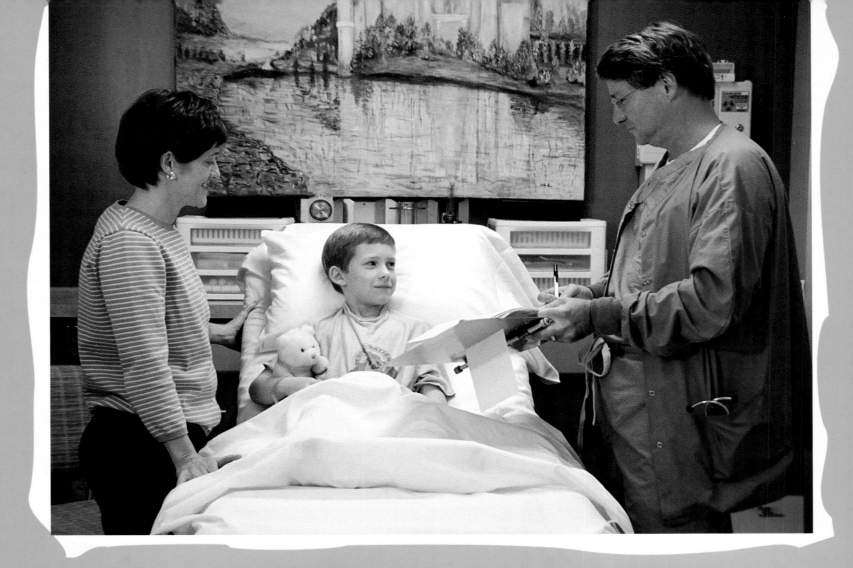

Meeting More Friends

You will also meet your Anesthesiologist or your CRNA (Certified Registered Nurse Anesthetist). They are responsible for helping you sleep comfortably during your surgery. They will have questions for you and your mom, dad, or special friend before you go to the operating room.

Your doctor may ask your anesthesia friend to get a small sample of blood to send to the lab. You will either have a quick finger prick ...

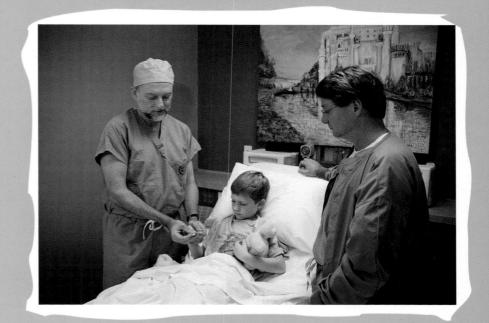

... or a needle is put into a vein in your hand or arm. Either way, this only hurts for a few seconds.

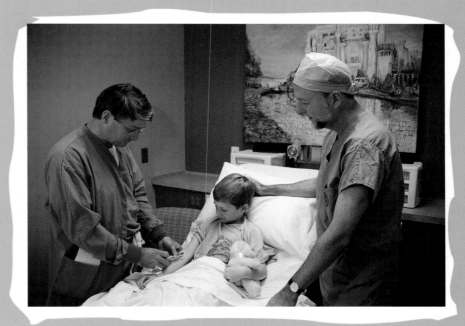

Talking to your Doctor

Before your surgery, your doctor will come by and introduce you and your mom, dad, or special friend to another nurse friend. This nurse friend will be taking care of you while you are in the operating room. If you have any questions about your surgery, ask your doctor or nurse friend for the answers. Once all your questions have been answered, you are ready to go to the operating room.

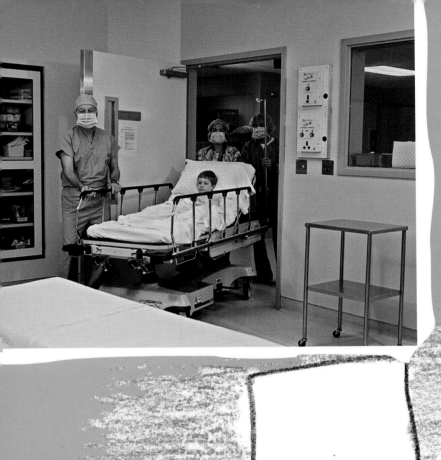

The Operating Room

You will notice that everyone in the operating room will be wearing scrub clothes, a special hat, shoe covers, and a mask over their nose and mouth. Scrub clothes are worn by everyone in the operating room during your surgery. They wear scrub clothes to make sure germs don't spread in the operating room.

Your Surgery

Your operating room nurse friend and anesthesia friend will be with you in the operating room during your surgery. Your parents are not allowed in the operating room, but your nurse friend will call them during your surgery and let them know how you are doing. The operating room can be a little cold sometimes. Tell your nurse friend if you are cold and she will give you a warm blanket.

Before your surgery starts, your nurse friend will place monitors on you. These monitors will tell your doctor how you are doing during your surgery. The first monitor is a blood pressure cuff, just like the one your pre-operative nurse friend put on your arm in your room.

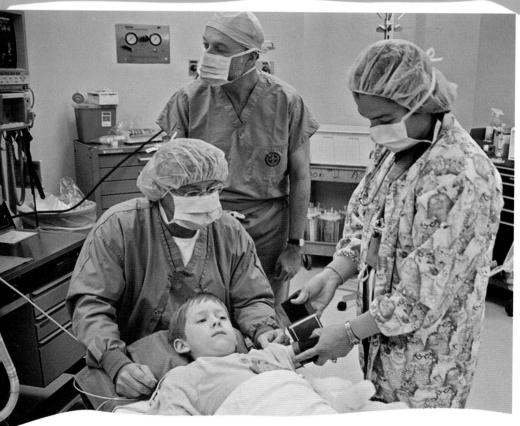

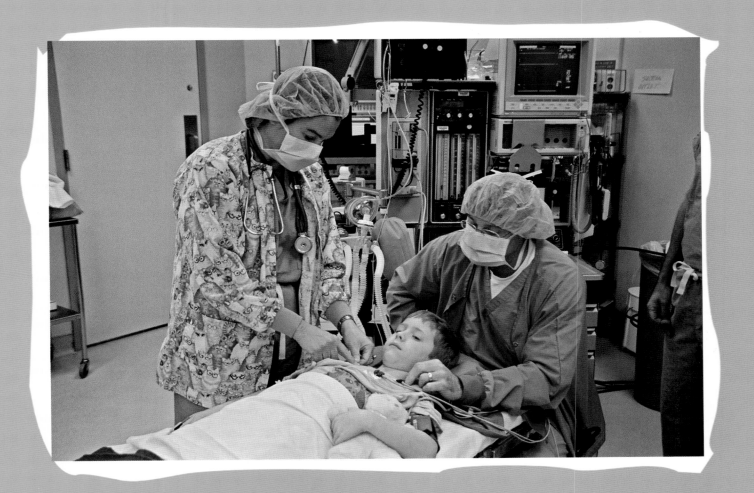

The second monitors that will be put on you are EKG (Electrocardiogram) pads. Your nurse friend will put EKG pads that are cold and sticky on your chest and back. EKG pads monitor your heart rate during your surgery.

The last monitor that will be used in the operating room is the pulse oximeter. The pulse oximeter will be clipped to your finger and will have a red light on the end of it. The pulse oximeter will not hurt your finger and will tell your anesthesia friend the tissue/oxygen levels in your body.

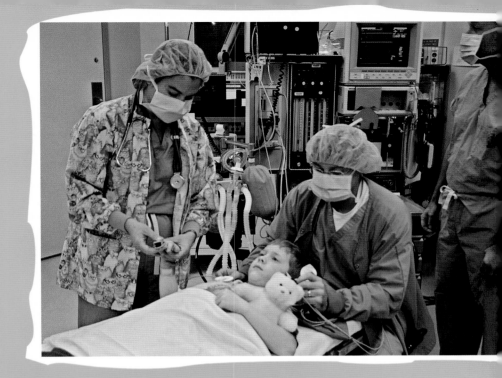

The last thing you have to do before your surgery is breathe through a mask. Your anesthesia friend will help you breathe gas through a mask. When you breathe through this mask, the gas may smell funny, but will make you fall asleep very quickly.

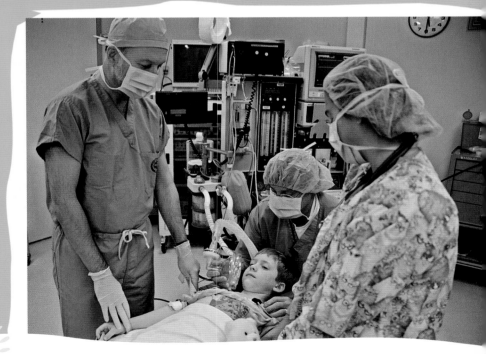

After you fall asleep, your anesthesia friend will put an IV (stands for intravenous) in the top of your hand or in your arm. Remember, you could not eat or drink anything before your surgery. The IV will provide liquid nourishment to your body. The liquids are in a bag connected to the tubing that will run into your arm or the top of your hand. The IV will be taped onto your hand to keep it from falling out. You can still move your hand and arm around after the IV has been put in. After your surgery is finished, you will be taken to the Recovery Room.

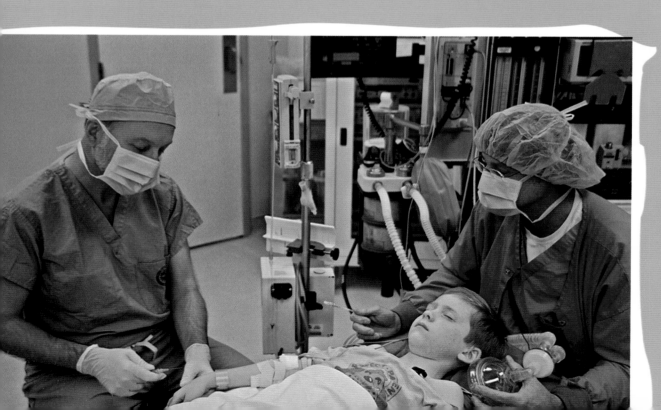

22

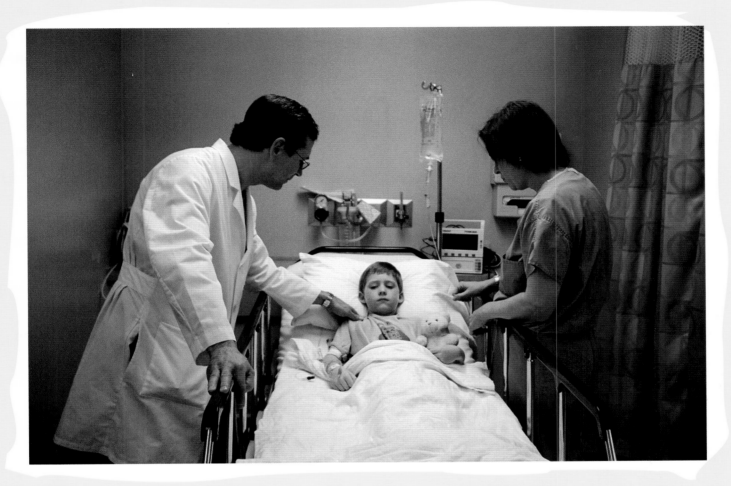

The Recovery Room

You will wake up after your surgery in the Recovery Room. You will have a new nurse friend that will take good care of you while you are there. When you wake up after your surgery, you will feel groggy and sleepy. If your stomach feels queezy or you feel pain when you wake up, make sure you tell your nurse friend. Your nurse friend will watch you closely and give you medicines that will make you feel much better. When you start waking up and begin to feel better, you will be taken to your post-operative room.

After your Surgery

Once you reach your post-operative room, you still will be very sleepy and tired. Your mom, dad, or special friend will meet you in your post-operative room. Try to sleep as much as possible and follow your doctor's and nurse friend's instructions. Sleep will help you recover much faster from your surgery.

If you need help going to the bathroom, changing clothes, or drinking liquids, your nurse friend will be there to help you. Before you leave to go home, your nurse friend will take the IV out of your hand or arm. When your IV is taken out of your hand or arm, it won't hurt. Your nurse friend will put a small bandage or band aid on the hand or arm where your IV was inserted.

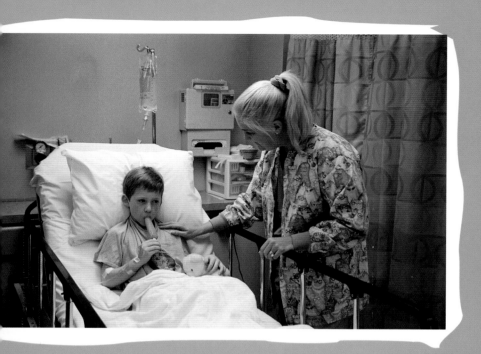

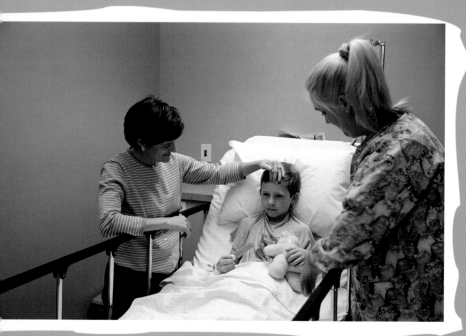

Going Home

Most outpatient surgery centers have a rule that you must ride in a wheelchair to your car after your surgery. Your nurse friend or another staff member will push you in a wheelchair to your parents' or special friends' car when you are ready to go home.

You're Home

Once you arrive home, there will be several instructions you must follow. Your mom, dad, or special friend can help you remember these instructions. First, you must get plenty of rest and sleep after your surgery. Rest and sleep will help you feel much better, so you can quickly return to playing with your friends and family.

Second, you must take the medicines your doctor has given you after your surgery. These medicines will help your body heal faster and feel better.

Follow your doctor's instructions and you will be able to do two things. The first thing you can do is return to playing with brothers, sisters, and friends.

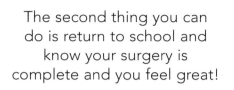

The second thing you can
do is return to school and
know your surgery is
complete and you feel great!

29

Your hospital experience

Your hospital experience

Drawings